A Christmas Story

A Christmas Story

BY

Jay Frankston

ILLUSTRATIONS BY PAUL BACON

SUMMIT BOOKS

NEW YORK

Published by *Summit Books*
A Simon & Schuster Division of Gulf & Western Corporation
Simon & Schuster Building
1230 Avenue of the Americas
New York, New York 10020
Designed by Paul Bacon
Manufactured in the United States of America
Printed by The Murray Printing Company
Bound by The Book Press
1   2   3   4   5   6   7   8   9   10

Library of Congress Cataloging in Publication Data

Frankston, Jay, date.
  A Christmas story.

  SUMMARY: The author describes how and why he became
Santa Claus each year to a number of needy children whose
letters to Santa he found in the postal service's dead
letter office.
  1. Santa Claus. [1. Christmas stories.] I. Bacon,
Paul, date. II. Title.
GT4992.F72A32   973.92′092′4 [B]   78-17995

ISBN 0-671-40066-5

The author intends
that the major portion
of the royalties
he derives from
this book go to
create a needy
children's foundation.

This little book
is dedicated
to my daughter,
Claire,
who was my
inspiration.

There's nothing so beautiful as a child's dream of Santa Claus. I know, I often had that dream. But I was Jewish and we didn't celebrate Christmas. It was everyone else's holiday and I felt left out . . . a big party I wasn't invited to. Snow fell like confetti from the sky, making the streets ready for the festivities. Stores glittered and shone with new decorations. People rushed about buying presents and exchanging greetings.

The reindeer clattered on my rooftop, but Santa came down someone else's chimney, leaving a snowflake in my eye. So I withdrew into my woolen scarves and mittens and looked out with envy from under my cap at all the excitement I was not part of. Christmas didn't belong to me. It wasn't the toys I yearned for, it was Santa Claus and a Christmas tree. So when I got married and had kids I decided to make up for what I'd missed.

I started with a seven-foot tree, all decked out with lights and tinsel. My daughter, Claire, was only two but her eyes sparkled as she smiled at it. It was more than just a tree, it was a presence in the house and it gave off warmth which filled every corner of our home. I put a Star of David on top to soothe those whose Jewish feelings were disturbed by the display and, for them, it was a Hanukkah bush. And it warmed my heart to see the glitter, because now the party was at *my* house and *everyone* was invited.

But something was missing, something big and round and jolly, with jingle bells and a ho! ho! ho! So I bought a bolt of bright red cloth and strips of white fur and my wife made me a costume. Inflatable pillows rounded out my skinny frame, but no amount of makeup could turn my face into merry old Santa.

I went around looking at department store impersonations sitting on their thrones with children on their laps and

flashbulbs going, and I wasn't satisfied with the way they looked either. After much effort, I located a mask maker and he had just the thing for me, a rubberized Santa mask, complete with whiskers and flowing white hair. It was not a real face but it looked genuine enough to live up to a child's dream of old St. Nick.

When I tried on the mask something happened. I looked in the mirror and there he was, big as life, the Santa of my childhood. There he was . . . and it was me. I felt myself becoming Santa. My posture changed. I leaned back and pushed out my pillow stomach. My head tilted to the side and my voice got deeper and richer. "Merry Christmas, everyone."

Claire was almost four and Danny not yet one when Santa first came to the house. They stood in awe and I saw in their eyes the fantasy and magic of what I had become. Santa was special.

He was more than the Tooth Fairy and the Easter Bunny. He was the personification of kindness and gentleness. He was a little scary too. He knew each one of them and knew them well. But he brought toys and made them smile, and their excitement lingered long after he left.

For two years I played Santa for my children to their mixed feelings of fright and delight and to my total enjoyment.

And when the third year rolled around, the Santa in me had grown into a personality of his own and he needed more room than I had given him. So I sought to accommodate him by letting him do his thing for other children. I called up orphanages and children's hospitals and offered his services free.

But, "We don't need Santa, we have all sorts of donations from foundations and . . . thank you for calling."

And the Santa in me felt lonely and useless.

Then, one late November afternoon, I went to the mailbox on the corner of the street and saw this pretty little girl trying to reach the slot. She was maybe six years old.

"Mommy, are you sure Santa will get my letter?" she asked.

"Well, you addressed it to Santa Claus, North Pole, so he should get it," the mother said and lifted her little girl who stuffed the letter into the box.

My mind began to whirl.

All those thousands of children who wrote to Santa Claus at Christmas time, whatever became of their letters? One phone call to the main post office answered my question. They told me that, as of the last week of November, an entire floor of the post office was needed to store those letters in huge sacks.

The Santa in me went ho! ho! ho! and we headed down to the post office.

And there they were, thousands upon thousands of letters, with or without stamps, addressed to Santa Claus, or St. Nick, or Kris Kringle, scribbled on wrapping paper or neatly written on pretty stationery.

And I rummaged through them and laughed. Most of them were gimme, gimme, gimme letters, like "I want a pair of roller skates, and a bicycle, and a GI Joe, and an etch-a-sketch, and a portable TV, and whatever else you can think of." Many of them had the price alongside each item . . . with or without sales tax.

Then there were the funny ones like "Dear Santa, I've been a good boy all of last year, but if I don't get what I want, I'll be a bad boy all of next."

And I became a little flustered at the demands and greed of so many spoiled children. But the Santa in me heard a voice from inside the mail sack and I continued going through the letters one after the other until I came upon one which jarred and unsettled me. It was neatly written on plain white paper and it said:

Dear Santa,
I hope you'll get my letter. I am an eleven year old girl and I have two little brothers and a baby sister. My father died last year and my mother is sick. I know there are many who are poorer than we are and I want nothing for myself but could you send us a blanket cause mommy's cold at night.

And a chill went up my spine and the Santa in me cried, "I hear you, Suzy, I hear you."

And I dug deeper into those sacks and came up with another eight such letters, all calling out from the depths of poverty. I took them with me and went straight to the nearest Western Union office and sent each child a telegram:

GOT YOUR LETTER. WILL BE AT YOUR HOUSE. WAIT FOR ME. SANTA.

I knew I could not possibly fill all the needs of these children and it wasn't my purpose to do so, but if I could bring them hope, if I could make them feel that their cries did not go unheard and that someone out there was listening . . .

So I budgeted $150 and went out and bought toys. I wasn't content with the five- and ten-cent variety. I wanted something substantial, something these children could only dream of, like an electric train, or a microscope, or a huge doll of the kind they saw advertised on TV.

And on Christmas Day I took out my sleigh and let Santa do his thing. It wasn't exactly a sleigh, it was a car, and my wife drove me around because with all those pillows and toys I barely managed to get in the back seat. It had graciously snowed the night before, and the streets were thick with fresh powder. My first call took me to the outskirts of the city. The letter had been from a Peter Barsky and all it said was

Dear Santa,

I am ten years old and I am an only child. We've just moved to this house a few months ago and I have no friends yet. I'm not sad because I'm poor but because I'm lonely. I know you have many things to do and people to see and you probably have no time for me. So I don't ask you to come to my house or bring anything but could you send me a letter so I know you exist.

Peter

My telegram read:

DEAR PETER, NOT ONLY DO I EXIST BUT I'LL BE THERE ON CHRISTMAS DAY. WAIT FOR ME.

We spotted the house and drove past it and parked around the corner. Then Santa got out with his big bag of toys slung over his shoulder and tramped through the snow.

The house was wedged between two tall buildings. Its roof was of corrugated metal and it was more of a shack than a house. I walked through the gate and up the front steps and rang the bell. A man opened the door. He was in his undershirt and his stomach bulged out of his pants.

"*Boje moy,*" he said in astonishment. That's Polish, by the way, and his hand went to his face. "Please—" he stuttered "please—the boy—the boy—at mass—church. I go get him. Please—please wait." And he threw a coat over his bare shoulders and, assured that I would wait, he ran down the street in the snow.

So I stood there in front of the house feeling good, and on the opposite side of the street was another shack, and through the window I could see shiny little black faces peering at me and waving.

Then the door opened shyly and some voices called out, "Hya, Santa . . . Hya, Santa."

And I ho! ho! hoed my way over there and this woman asked if I'd come in and I did. And there were five young kids from one to seven years old. And I sat and spoke to them of Santa and the spirit of love which is the spirit of Christmas. Then, since they were not on my list, but assuming from the torn Christmas wrappings that they had gotten their presents, I asked if they liked what Santa had brought them during the night. And each in turn thanked me, for the woolen socks, and the sweater, and the warm new underwear.

I looked at them. "Didn't I bring you kids any toys?"

And they shook their heads sadly.

"Ho! ho! ho! I slipped up," I said. "We'll have to fix that." I told them to wait, I'd be back in a few minutes, then trudged heavily through the snow to the corner.

And when I was out of sight, I ran as fast as I could to the car.

We had extra toys in the trunk. My wife quickly filled up the bag, and I tramped back to the house and gave each child a brand-new toy. There was joy and laughter and the woman asked my permission to take a picture of Santa with the kids and I said, sure, why not?

And when Santa got ready to leave, I noticed that this five-year-old little girl was crying. She was as cute as a button. I bent down and asked her, "What's the matter, child?"

And she sobbed, "Oh, Santa! I'm so happy."

And the tears rolled from my eyes under the rubber mask.

As I stepped out on the street, *"Pan, pan, proche . . .* please come. . . come," I heard Mr. Barsky across the way. And Santa crossed and walked into the house.

The boy Peter just stood there and looked at me.

"You came," he said. "I wrote and—you came." He turned to his parents. "I wrote—and he came." And he repeated it over and over. "I wrote—and he came."

And when he recovered, I spoke with him about loneliness and friendship, and gave him a chemistry set, which seemed to be what he would go for, and a basketball. He thanked me profusely. And his mother, a heavy-set Slavic-looking woman, asked something of her husband in Polish. Since my parents were Polish, I speak a little and understand a lot.

"From the North Pole," I said in Polish.

She looked at me with astonishment. "You speak Polish?" she asked.

"Of course," I said. "Santa speaks all languages." And I left them in joy and wonder.

And the following year, when the momentum of Christmas began to build, I felt a stirring inside me and I knew that Santa was back. So I returned to the post office and to those letters—those heartbreaking letters.

And when I shopped for toys, the manager of the toy department of a large downtown store asked me how many children I had, because I bought so many things.

When I told him what I was doing, he
started by letting me have twenty per-
cent off. Then he told me he could give
me twenty-dollar toys for a dollar or
two, if I didn't mind that the wrapping
was broken. I waited while he collected
a number of toys, but there weren't
enough. So he scratched his head
for a moment, reached for some large
dolls on the open shelf and went into
a corner. Then he looked around as
though he didn't want anyone else
to see him, punched out the plastic
wrapper and, turning back to me,
said, "Here, *these* are broken packages
too." And a warm feeling came over me.

By the 23rd of December I was ready.
The toys were gift-wrapped with ribbons
and bows, the names of the children
were on each one, the itinerary was laid
out . . . but it hadn't snowed yet. Snow,
snow, Santa had to have snow. He
couldn't deliver Christmas on bare
cement pavements. So I prayed for snow.
And in the morning, the streets were
covered. I guess someone up there heard
me, and it was always a white Christmas.

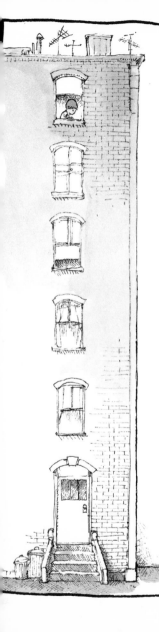

W e drove from
one section of the city to
another, making our
stops. And in between,
Santa sat heavily in the
back seat, waving at
children in other cars
and on the street.

When we got to the
inner part of the city,
my wife stayed in the
car while I went into
the building where a
child named Billy lived.
There were cockroaches
on the walls and rats on
the stairs. I climbed six
flights, sweating
heavily under the suit,
and knocked on the
door.

And when it was opened, it opened on warmth and close family life. The place was small but so clean you could eat off the floor.

Billy was six years old and his letter had said: "Santa, I love you no matter what my brother says." And Billy had a mouthful of smiles. But his brother was nine and already a skeptic. His wall was thick and mortared with street experience, and he kept his doors and windows locked. But every door has its key, you just have to find it. So Santa told jokes that made him laugh, and the wall came tumbling down.

Most of the children got to see Santa only once but my children were privileged. I continued playing Santa for them and they got used to seeing him every year. They waited for him anxiously, for he was now a warm and familiar figure. Still, I had to use many tricks to keep them believing.

A
nd when she was ten, Claire handed me a poem which read:

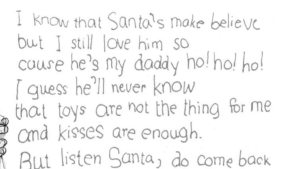

I know that Santa's make believe
but I still love him so
cause he's my daddy ho! ho! ho!
I guess he'll never know
that toys are not the thing for me
and kisses are enough.
But listen Santa, do come back
and bring instead of toys
a package full of hugs and kisses
made for girls and boys.
Now you make sure to make them nice
especially for me
Or I will never ever want
to sit on Santa's knee.

So now she knew. And I took her down to the basement where the toys were lined up from floor to ceiling and let her rummage through Santa's shop, marveling wide-eyed at the imposing array. She read the letters and cried with me and became a true Santa's helper, sorting the gifts and re-wrapping the toys in preparation for my rounds.

And I made those rounds for twelve years, going through the letters to Santa at the post office, listening for the cries of children muffled in unopened envelopes, letters from children who were often past the age of believing, yet wrote a last farewell to Santa Claus, to childhood, and to hope . . . answering the call of as many as I could and frustrated at not being able to answer them all.

But Santa was full of joy in the giving and in time I learned all that Santa has to know to handle any situation. Like the big kid who would stop Santa on the street and ask, "Hey, Santa, where's your sleigh?"

And I'd say, "How
old are you, son?"
  And he'd say, "Thirteen."
  And I'd say, "Well,
you're a big fellow and
you ought to know
better. Santa used to come
in a sleigh many years ago,
but these are modern times.
I come in a car now."
And I'd hop in the back seat
and my wife would drive off.
  Or the kid who would
look at me closely and
come out with, "That's
a mask," pointing a finger.
And I'd say, "Sure, son, of course.

If everybody knew what Santa really looks like they'd bother me all year long and I couldn't get my things ready for Christmas."

Or the mother who would whisper to me so her young son couldn't hear, "Where do you come from?"

I'd turn to the child and say, "Your mom wants to know where I come from, Willy."

And he'd say, "From the North Pole, Mommy," with absolute certainty.

And she'd nudge me and whisper, "You don't understand. Who sent you? I mean, how do you come to *this* house?"

I'd turn to the boy and say, "Hey, Willy, your mom wants to know why I came to see you."

And he'd say, "Cause I wrote him a letter, Mommy."

And I'd pull out the letter and she'd know she'd mailed it, and she'd be confused and bewildered and I'd leave her like that.

As time went on, the word got out about Santa Claus and me, and I insisted on anonymity, but toy manufacturers would send me huge cartons of toys as a contribution to the Christmas spirit. So I started with 18 or 20 children and wound up with 120, door to door, from one end of the city to the other, from Christmas Eve through Christmas Day.

And on my last call, a few years ago, I knew there were four children in the family and I came prepared.

The house was small and sparsely furnished. The kids had been waiting all day, staring at the telegram and repeating to their skeptical mother, "He'll come, Mommy, he'll come."

And as I rang the door bell the house lit up with joy and laughter and "He's here . . . he's here!" And the door swings open and they all reach for my hands and hold on. "Hya, Santa . . . Hya, Santa. We just knew you'd come." And these poor kids are all beaming with happiness.

And I take each one of them on my lap and speak to them of rainbows and snowflakes, and tell them stories of hope and waiting, and give them each a toy. And all the while there's this fifth child standing in the corner, a cute little girl with blond hair and blue eyes.

And when I'm through with the others, I turn to her and say, "You're not part of this family, are you?"

And she shakes her head sadly and whispers, "No."

"Come closer, child," I say, and she comes a little closer.

"What's your name?" I ask.

"Lisa."

"How old are you?"

"Seven."

"Come, sit on my lap," and she hesitates but she comes over and I lift her up and sit her on my lap.

"Did you get any toys for Christmas?" I ask.

"No," she says with puckered lips.

So I take out this big beautiful doll and, "Here, do you want this doll?"

"No," she says. And she leans over to me and whispers in my ear, "I'm Jewish."

And I nudge her and whisper in her ear, "I'm Jewish, too. Do you want this doll?"

And she's grinning from ear to ear and nods "Oh! Yes," and takes the doll and hugs it, and runs out.

Many years have passed since I last put on my Santa suit. But I feel that Santa has lived with me and given me a great deal of happiness all those years. And now, when Christmas rolls around, he comes out of hiding long enough to say, "Ho! ho! ho! A merry Christmas to you, my friend."

And I say to you now

Merry

Christmas,

My

Friends

A TRUE STORY

ABOUT THE AUTHOR

•

J AY FRANKSTON

and his wife, Monique,

now live in Little River,

a small coastal village

in northern California.

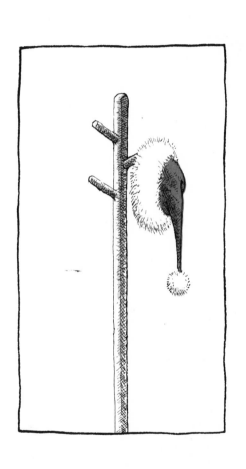